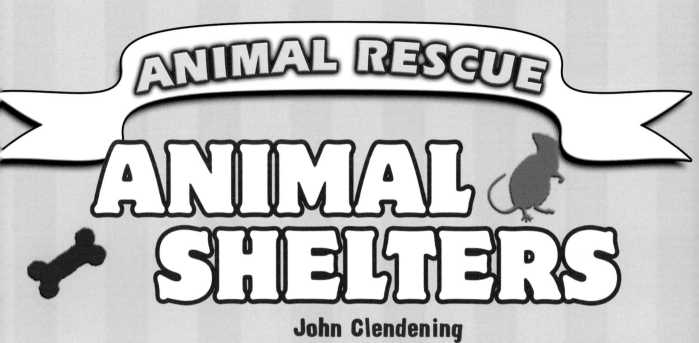

ANIMAL RESCUE

ANIMAL SHELTERS

John Clendening

PowerKiDS
press.
New York

Published in 2015 by The Rosen Publishing Group, Inc.
29 East 21st Street, New York, NY 10010

First Edition

Produced for Rosen by Cyan Candy, LLC
Editor: Joshua Shadowens
Designer: Erica Clendening, Cyan Candy

Photo Credits: Cover, pp. 8, 11, 15, 17, 18, 19, 20, 21, 23, 25, 27, 28, 29, 30 Shutterstock.com; p. 5 Wikimedia Commons; p. 7 Galawebdesign, via Wikimedia Commons; p. 9 Chatchai Somwat/Shutterstock.com; pp. 12, 13, 14 a katz/Shutterstock.com; p. 24 Leonard Zhukovsky/ Shutterstock.com.

Library of Congress Cataloging-in-Publication Data

Clendening, John.
 Animal shelters / by John Clendening. — First edition.
    pages cm. — (Animal rescue)
 Includes index.
 ISBN 978-1-4777-7011-5 (library binding) — ISBN 978-1-4777-7012-2 (pbk.) —
 ISBN 978-1-4777-7013-9 (6-pack)
 1. Animal shelters—Juvenile literature. I. Title.
 HV4708.C54 2015
 636.08'32—dc23

                                  2013047736

Manufactured in the United States of America

CPSIA Compliance Information: Batch #WS14PK8: For Further Information contact Rosen Publishing, New York, New York at 1-800-237-9932

TABLE OF CONTENTS

ANIMAL SHELTERS

Animal shelters are places that provide temporary homes for **homeless** animals that people keep as pets. They provide a safe and caring place for animals to live until they can find permanent homes. Animals need food, water, shelter, and medical care just like people do. Every day, homeless animals are brought to shelters, but there is not always enough space or money to feed and take care of them all.

Animal shelters try to find permanent homes for homeless animals through **adoption** programs, but not all animals get adopted. Sadly, due to overcrowding in shelters, some animals are **euthanized**, or put to sleep, if they cannot find new homes.

Over the years, animal shelters have been able to reduce the number of animals that are euthanized. Public education about responsible pet ownership and more human compassion towards animals have helped achieve this result.

There are many beautiful dogs all over the world right now living in animal shelters.

Most of the animals found in animal shelters today are cats and dogs, because these are the most popular types of pets. Some shelters also take care of other kinds of pet animals, like birds, reptiles, and rodents like rabbits, guinea pigs, mice, and rats.

There are animal shelters all over the world wherever people live. There is probably an animal shelter in your community full of animals right now that need new and loving, permanent places to call home!

These dogs may look sad, but those droopy ears serve a purpose. Basset Hounds have extra skin around their ears to help trap smells, which makes them excellent hunting dogs.

Black cats have historically been considered bad luck in many cultures throughout history. Because of this, black cats today are often the last to be adopted in many shelters.

Animal Rescue!

It is estimated that 7 out of 10 American households have a dog or a cat as a pet. There are about 314 million people in the United States today, which means that there are about 220 million cats and dogs living with people as pets in America.

WHY WE NEED ANIMAL SHELTERS

There are a lot of animals in the world! Many of them become homeless and need to live in shelters for different reasons. Sometimes people die and there is nobody else to take care of their pet. Other times, people have financial problems and can no longer afford to take care

Volunteering at an animal shelter can be a very rewarding experience. Shelter dogs need to be fed, taken for walks, and played with just like animals with permanent homes do.

of an animal. Some animals are brought to shelters if they bite or hurt someone. This can make people afraid to let the pet continue to live in their house.

Sometimes pets run away and become lost. If they are found by someone who does not know where the pet lives, the animal may be brought to a shelter so it can be helped. Animals are also brought to shelters following natural disasters, fires, and floods.

Following natural disasters, people and animals need lots of help. This person and a dog needed help getting across a flooded street in Bangkok, Thailand, after a devastating monsoon.

Some people don't want their pet anymore and let the pet go free instead of bringing it to a shelter. This can pose a risk to people and other animals living in the area. **Domesticated** animals can quickly become **feral** when they are left to fend for their own survival and no longer have humans to take care of them.

Shelters are needed to help prevent animals from becoming a danger to people and to other animals. Housing and caring for them properly until they can find new homes is the main function of animal shelters.

Animal Rescue!

Dogs can form hunting packs to increase their odds of survival when they become homeless. Packs can be dangerous to people or other animals. Cats are solitary hunters and do not form packs. However, homeless cats can also pose risks to humans. Feral cats can sometimes transmit diseases to humans if they bite or scratch them.

Borzoi dogs have been bred to maximize their naturally strong hunting instincts and skills. They were brought to Russia from Central Asia many years ago. In Russian, *borzoi* means "fast."

TYPES OF SHELTERS AND HOW THEY'RE MADE

There are two basic types of animal shelters, public and private. Public shelters are operated by local governments. They are **funded** and created using money from **taxes** that all citizens pay. Private shelters are created, funded, and operated without public tax money, using private sources of money such as **donations**.

Shelters can also be classified as kill or no-kill shelters. In a kill shelter, animals are sometimes euthanized after a set number of days if nobody comes looking for them,

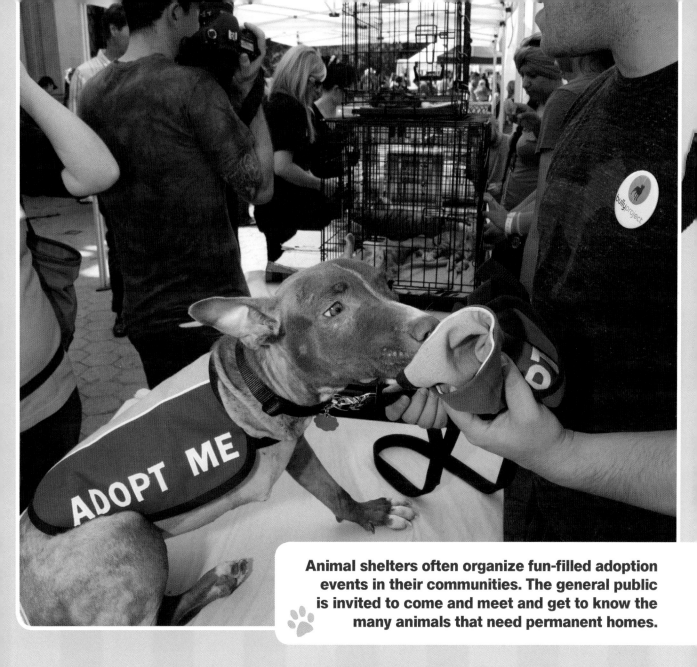

Animal shelters often organize fun-filled adoption events in their communities. The general public is invited to come and meet and get to know the many animals that need permanent homes.

if they become too sick, get badly injured and cannot be saved, or if nobody wants to adopt them.

In overcrowded shelters, animals can sometimes be euthanized in as few as 7–14 days. In no-kill shelters, healthy and adoptable animals are never euthanized. Animals in most of these shelters are cared for until they are adopted or die of old age.

Every community has homeless animals and needs a public animal shelter. Because public shelters often do not have enough money, they cannot help every animal. People who care a lot about helping animals create private shelters to try to help the animals that public shelters cannot help and to prevent animals from being euthanized.

Private shelters can be multi-million dollar, state-of-the-art facilities, or they can be very small and located within a single family home. No matter how big or small a shelter is they all exist to try to help as many homeless animals as they can.

A volunteer at the Broadway Barks adoption event in New York City. Celebrities are invited to make adoption events more exciting so more people will come and adopt more pets.

Animal Rescue!

People have to pay taxes because governments need money for many different things that communities need, like police and fire departments, roads, schools, and hospitals. In some communities, little tax money is left over to operate animal shelters in a way that allows them to help all of the animals that need help.

THE ORIGINS OF ANIMAL SHELTERS

Animal shelters used to be called pounds. They were created to temporarily house **livestock** and work animals like cows and horses that got loose from ranches and farms. Ranchers and farmers could reclaim their animals from pounds by paying a fee to the pound master. Since ranch and farm animals were valuable to their owners, most pound animals were claimed.

Compared to bigger animals that people considered more valuable and useful, cats and dogs brought to pounds were usually not claimed by anyone and would typically be euthanized.

Animal Rescue!

Livestock animals like cows, goats, pigs, and sheep have long been considered valuable to humans. People use these animals for meat and for their milk. Animal fur and skins are used for clothing. Work animals, such as horses and donkeys, help people get difficult work done because they are big and strong.

Before we had engines, horses worked hard for people. We compared how much work engines did to how much work horses did. This is where the word "horsepower" comes from.

Cats and dogs have lived with people for thousands of years but were not always as popular as household pets as they are today. Before the early 1900s, most people lived in the country. When many people began leaving the countryside and moving into cities, cats and dogs started to become more popular as pets. Due to their small size, compared to bigger animals, they are easier to take care of and share a home with, especially in cities where people generally have less living space than they did when living in the country.

People take care of their pets but pets can help people too. Did you know that simply petting a cat can help people relax and lower a person's stress level?

This dog barely has any room in this cage he has to share with other dogs. Surely it would prefer living in a home with more room to move around.

As dogs and cats became more popular as pets, their populations grew, which caused them to become the most common animals needing shelters. As a result, shelters became populated mostly with dogs and cats, and not with livestock and work animals like they were in the past.

SHELTER ANIMALS

Before the 1970s, shelter animal populations were very high, and as a result, about 100 out of every 1,000 shelter animals were euthanized. Towards the end of the 1970s, public concern about high euthanasia rates inspired a shelter in Los Angeles, California, to create the first low-cost **spay** and **neuter** clinic.

Sterilization, which is a fast and painless medical operation, prevents animals from reproducing. As shelters and **veterinarians** performed more of these operations, cat and dog populations began to decline. This led to lower shelter populations and fewer animals being euthanized.

Left: Animals need doctor checkups and sometimes medicine to make sure they are healthy.
Right: Many animals do not like visiting a veterinarian office, but it is important to take them anyway.

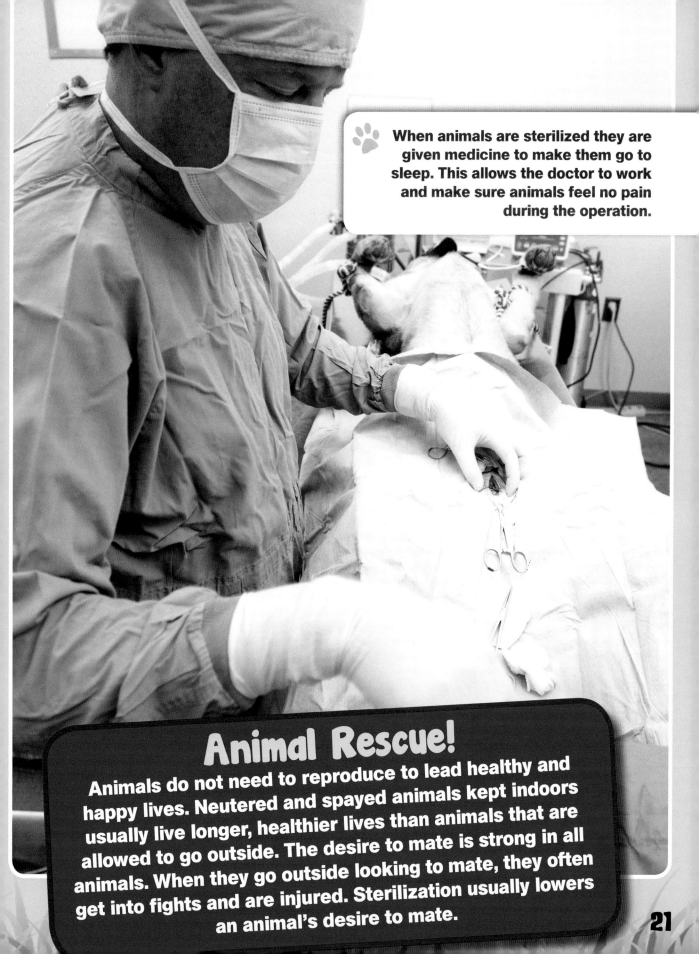

When animals are sterilized they are given medicine to make them go to sleep. This allows the doctor to work and make sure animals feel no pain during the operation.

Animal Rescue!

Animals do not need to reproduce to lead healthy and happy lives. Neutered and spayed animals kept indoors usually live longer, healthier lives than animals that are allowed to go outside. The desire to mate is strong in all animals. When they go outside looking to mate, they often get into fights and are injured. Sterilization usually lowers an animal's desire to mate.

Puppies and kittens need veterinarian care to ensure that they grown up healthy. Before the 1990s, most young pets would only get a veterinarian checkup and shots to immunize them against diseases as they grew. By the 1990s, spaying and neutering had become routine, and people had to opt out, or request, that their pets not be sterilized. Animal shelters had finally found a way to help reduce the suffering of animals due to overcrowding in shelters, and the euthanasia that sometimes became necessary due to the overcrowding.

As a result, euthanasia rates dropped to 10 percent of the levels seen before the 1970s. That is down from 100 of every 1,000 animals, to 12.5 of every 1,000 animals. The success of sterilization programs sparked a national debate about other ways to decrease shelter populations and the number of shelter animals being euthanized.

Veterinarians are trained to notice many important things about an animal's health just by looking at and touching an animal. It can be a very rewarding career for animal lovers.

ANIMAL SHELTERS TODAY AND IN THE FUTURE

There is currently no federal oversight of animal shelter operations in the United States. Accurate statistics do not exist that can tell us things like exactly how many animals are currently in shelters, and how many are euthanized each year. It could be helpful to have national standards so that people could have better information to use to

ASPCA logo

Animal Rescue!

The ASPCA estimates that 60 percent of the 8–10 million shelter animals in the United States are euthanized each year. The Humane Society estimates that same number to be 50 percent. Both figures are only estimates since there is no way to be sure without a national program to oversee shelters and gather the information.

Cats and dogs have multiple babies when they give birth. Most people do not want that many animals to take care of so many baby animals end up in shelters.

address the needs of shelter animals. The two largest animal shelter organizations in the United States are the American Society for the Prevention of Cruelty to Animals (ASPCA) and the Humane Society of the United States (Humane Society).

Animal shelters today are generally much nicer and more comfortable places for homeless animals to call home than they were in the past. No longer just basic, uncomfortable, and visually unattractive concrete pens surrounded by fences. Many modern shelters try to really make animals happy while they are there. Some create rooms for each animal that look and feel just like a room in a person's house, with a bed or a couch, rugs, natural sunlight, fresh air, and sometimes even relaxing music.

Happier and more relaxed animals are healthier which can make them more adoptable. The goal of shelters has never been to have the animals living there be miserable. By being more creative and thinking of ways to make animals happier and more comfortable in shelters, shelter staff can continue to improve the lives of the animals they care for.

Dogs are intelligent animals, and they need exercise and stimulation to be happy and healthy. Dogs like to play with toys and to play games just like human beings do.

FINAL THOUGHTS

There have been many positive advances over the years in the shelter system but millions of animals still end up in shelters and many are still euthanized each year. The number of US households with dogs or cats as pets has doubled over the past 40 years. Between 1973 and 2007, pet populations doubled, but euthanasia rates dropped more than 60 percent.

This trend shows us that if we as a society spend more money on shelters, and particularly on spay and neuter programs, we can control the pet population to

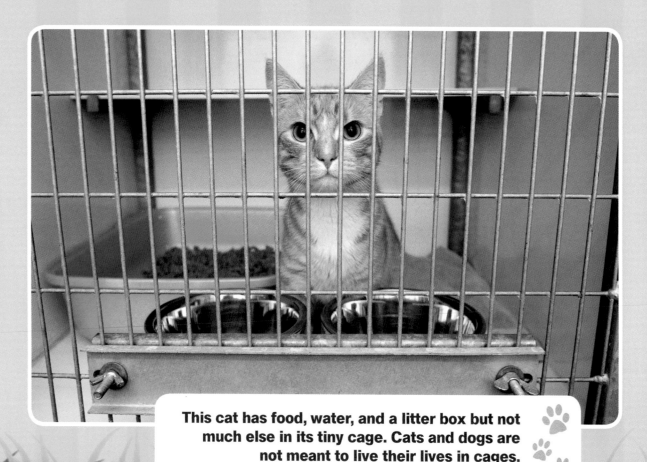

This cat has food, water, and a litter box but not much else in its tiny cage. Cats and dogs are not meant to live their lives in cages.

more manageable levels and lower euthanasia rates. A common goal has emerged in our society: No healthy, adoptable animal should ever be euthanized. Volunteering at an animal shelter is one way to help animals. Shelters always need volunteers who care about animals.

Perhaps the best way to help a homeless animal is to give it a loving, permanent home. There are few reasons to buy a cat or a dog. Some people **breed** animals to sell them for money. Buying animals tells breeders that they should breed more animals to be sold.

With so many animals in shelters that need good homes, adopting one from a shelter is an excellent choice and can save an animal from living in a shelter. Most animals would probably love to live with a family who will treat them as a member of the family forever.

Weimaraner puppy

GLOSSARY

adoption (uh-DOP-shun) Taking an animal into your home to become your pet.

breed (BREED) To bring a male and a female animal together so they will have babies.

domesticated (duh-MES-tih-kayt-ed) Raised to live with people.

donations (doh-NAY-shunz) Gifts of money or help, contributions.

euthanized (YOO-thuh-nyzd) To put an animal to sleep, to kill.

feral (FER-al) An animal that used to live with humans but that has gone back to the wild.

funded (FUND-ed) To provide funds for.

homeless (HOHM-les) To have no home or permanent place of residence.

livestock (LYV-stok) Animals raised by people.

neuter (NOO-tur) To fix so that a male animal cannot make babies.

packs (PAKS) Groups of the same kind of animals hunting or living together.

spay (SPAY) To fix a female animal so that it cannot have babies.

sterilization (ster-ee-lih-ZAY-shun) To make incapable of reproduction.

taxes (TAKS-ez) Money added to the price of something or paid to a government for community services.

veterinarians (veh-tuh-ruh-NER-ee-unz) Doctors who treat animals.

INDEX

WEBSITES

Due to the changing nature of Internet links, PowerKids Press has developed an online list of websites related to the subject of this book. This site is updated regularly. Please use this link to access the list: **www.powerkids.com/ares/shelt/**